AF270374

HIGH-STAKES HEISTS

TRAIN HEISTS

KENNY ABDO

Fly!
An Imprint of Abdo Zoom
abdobooks.com

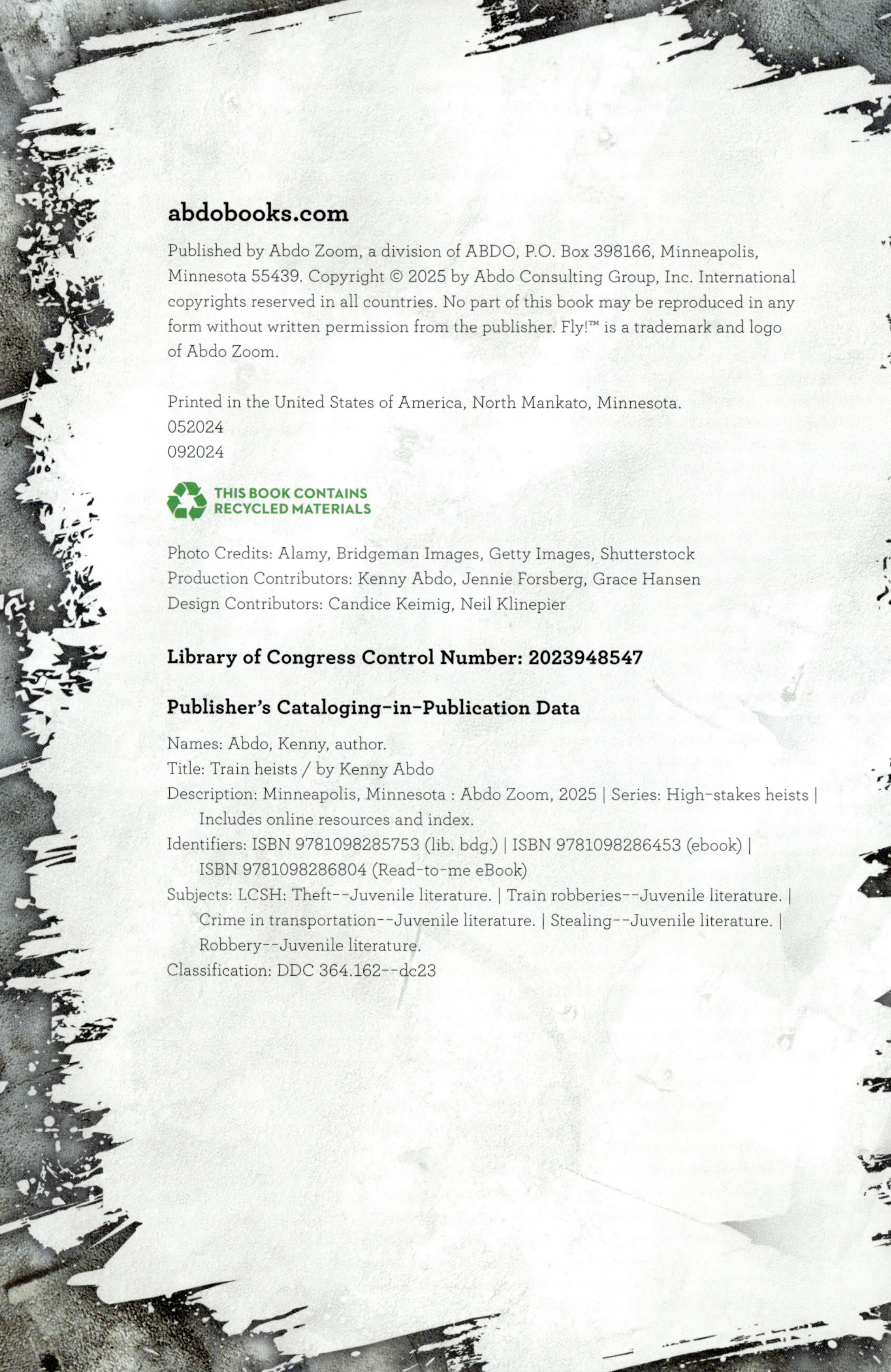

abdobooks.com

Published by Abdo Zoom, a division of ABDO, P.O. Box 398166, Minneapolis, Minnesota 55439. Copyright © 2025 by Abdo Consulting Group, Inc. International copyrights reserved in all countries. No part of this book may be reproduced in any form without written permission from the publisher. Fly!™ is a trademark and logo of Abdo Zoom.

Printed in the United States of America, North Mankato, Minnesota.
052024
092024

THIS BOOK CONTAINS RECYCLED MATERIALS

Photo Credits: Alamy, Bridgeman Images, Getty Images, Shutterstock
Production Contributors: Kenny Abdo, Jennie Forsberg, Grace Hansen
Design Contributors: Candice Keimig, Neil Klinepier

Library of Congress Control Number: 2023948547

Publisher's Cataloging-in-Publication Data

Names: Abdo, Kenny, author.
Title: Train heists / by Kenny Abdo
Description: Minneapolis, Minnesota : Abdo Zoom, 2025 | Series: High-stakes heists | Includes online resources and index.
Identifiers: ISBN 9781098285753 (lib. bdg.) | ISBN 9781098286453 (ebook) | ISBN 9781098286804 (Read-to-me eBook)
Subjects: LCSH: Theft--Juvenile literature. | Train robberies--Juvenile literature. | Crime in transportation--Juvenile literature. | Stealing--Juvenile literature. | Robbery--Juvenile literature.
Classification: DDC 364.162--dc23

TABLE OF CONTENTS

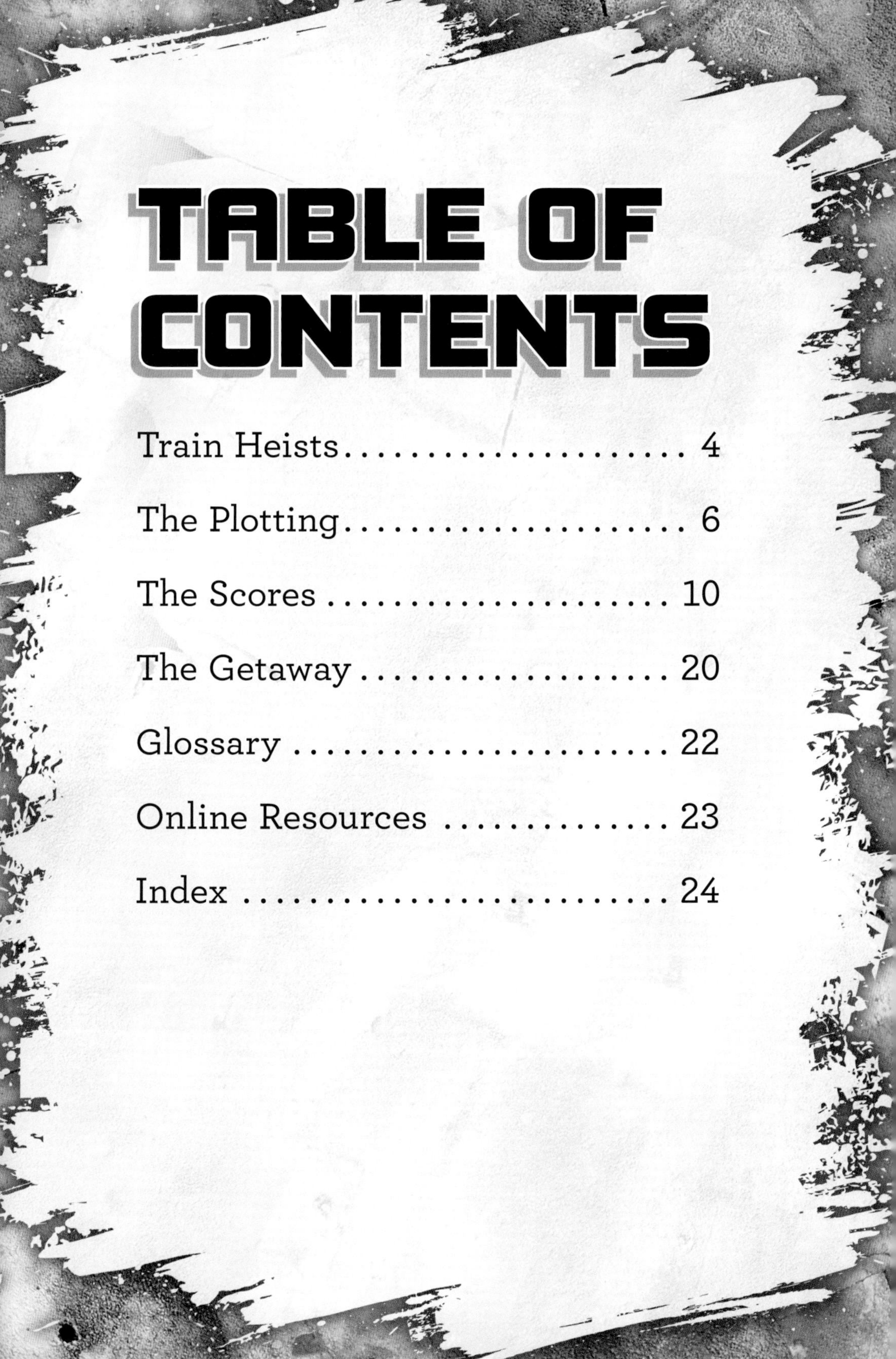

TRAIN HEISTS

The train changed the world for the better. Trains helped people and **goods** travel great distances swiftly, making them perfect targets for quick heists.

THE PLOTTING

In 1804, British inventor Richard Trevithick **debuted** his first railway **locomotive**. Soon, trains and railways would be seen throughout the world.

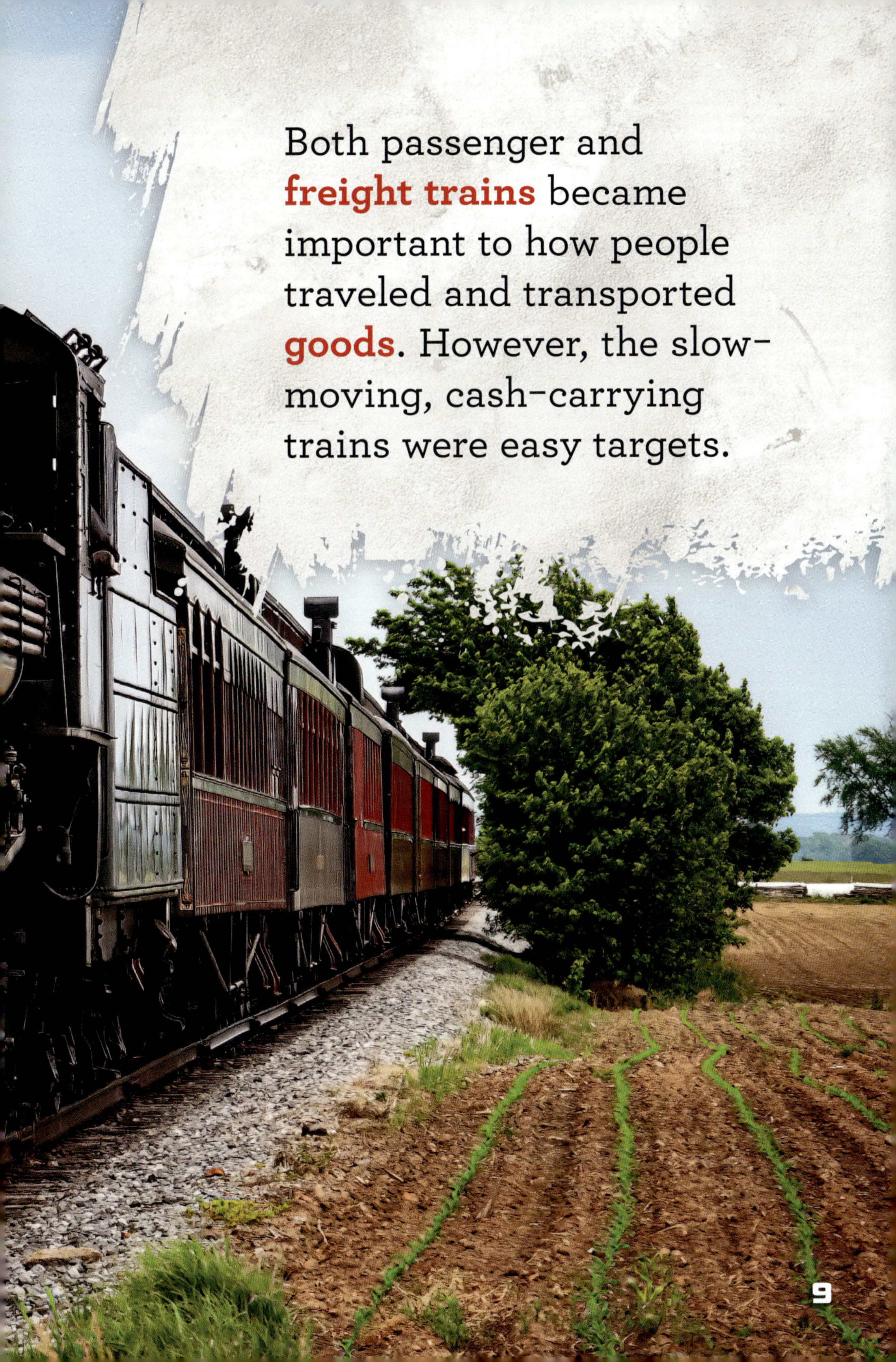

Both passenger and **freight trains** became important to how people traveled and transported **goods**. However, the slow-moving, cash-carrying trains were easy targets.

THE SCORES

In 1855, a train carrying gold bars from London to Paris was robbed. The thieves boarded the train and replaced the gold with **lead shots** without anyone noticing. They got away with the **equivalent** of $15,000 worth of gold.

The Verdi Train Robbery in California was a famous heist in 1870. Five men boarded a train carrying $60,000 worth of gold and silver. The gang was **apprehended** shortly after. Most of the loot was eventually recovered.

Jesse James and his gang committed an **infamous** robbery in 1873 in Iowa. They tied a rope to a track near a train station. The rail was jerked out of place, toppling the engine over. The gang escaped with nearly $3,000. That is worth about $51,000 today!

SITE OF THE FIRST TRAIN ROBBERY
IN THE WEST, COMMITTED BY
THE NOTORIOUS JESSE JAMES
AND HIS GANG OF OUTLAWS
JULY 21, 1873

A Santa Fe passenger train was targeted twice in just over a year. The Dalton Gang first attacked it in 1891, stealing $1,500. The second heist occurred in 1892. The thieves **fled** with more than $70,000 in cash.

Two lawmen-turned-**outlaws** attacked an express train in Arizona in 1899. They stole more than $10,000. When the robbery was reported, the two men pretended to search for the thieves.

Butch Cassidy and his Wild Bunch stuck up a train in 1901 in Montana. The **outlaws** shared a take of $40,000. That is worth more than $1 million today!

The Great Train Robbery of 1912 was the fastest in American history. Four robbers snatched $7,000 from a train in Oklahoma. They emptied the safe and escaped before the passengers knew. A manhunt was launched, but the gang was never caught.

Two men boarded a Southern Pacific train in Texas in 1937. They demanded money from the riders. However, they lost control of the situation and were arrested. The failed heist is considered the last major American train robbery.

A gang of thieves stole a lot of money from a London bound Royal Mail Train in 1963. Police found the men hiding in a farmhouse and sentenced them to 307 years in prison. The **equivalent** of $74 million stolen remains the largest in British history.

THE
GETAWAY

Trains have been important in keeping society chugging along. But with large stretches of land and little security, robbers have easily made some **ill-fated** trains go off the rails!

GLOSSARY

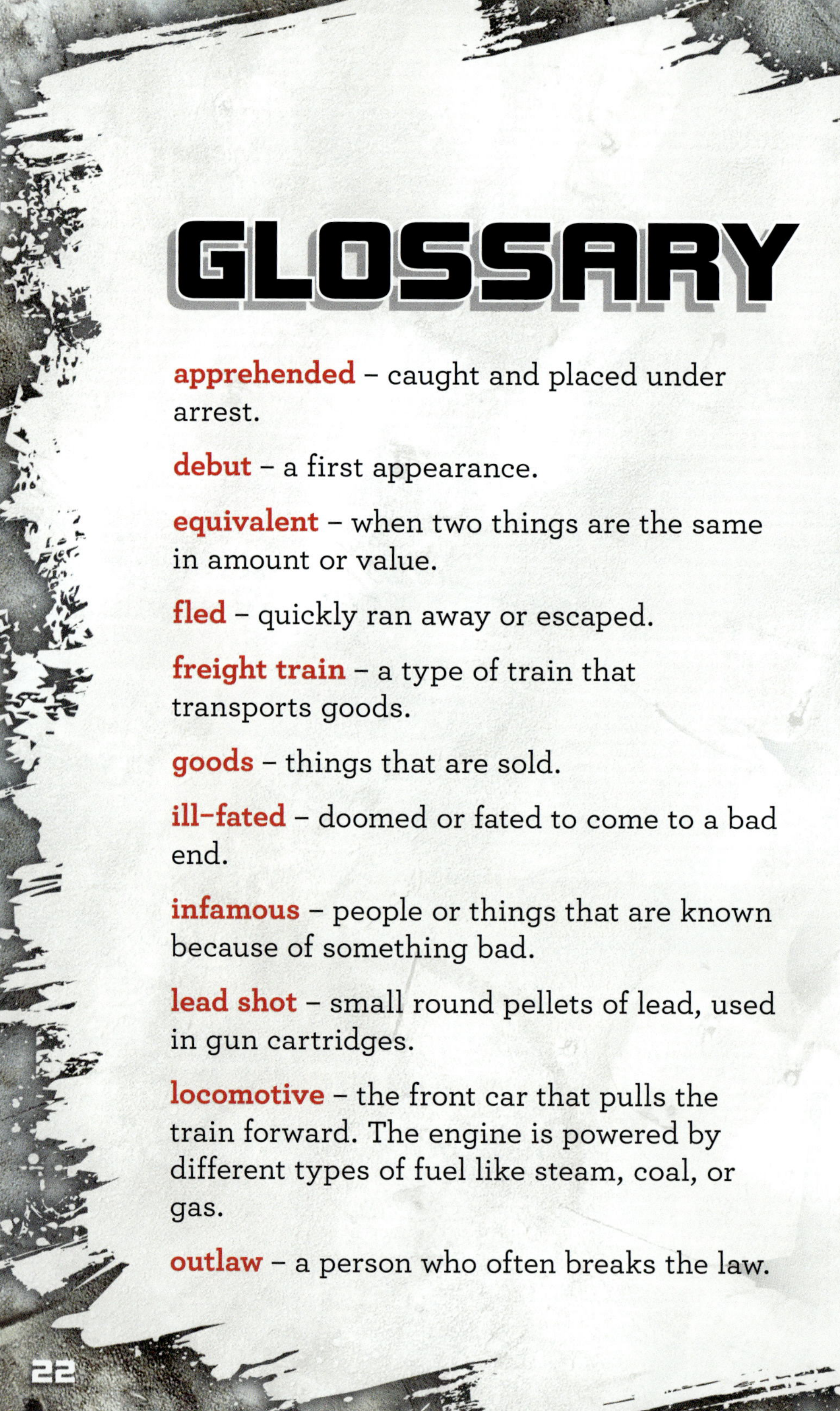

apprehended – caught and placed under arrest.

debut – a first appearance.

equivalent – when two things are the same in amount or value.

fled – quickly ran away or escaped.

freight train – a type of train that transports goods.

goods – things that are sold.

ill-fated – doomed or fated to come to a bad end.

infamous – people or things that are known because of something bad.

lead shot – small round pellets of lead, used in gun cartridges.

locomotive – the front car that pulls the train forward. The engine is powered by different types of fuel like steam, coal, or gas.

outlaw – a person who often breaks the law.

ONLINE RESOURCES
Booklinks
NONFICTION NETWORK
FREE! ONLINE NONFICTION RESOURCES
To learn more about train heists, please visit abdobooklinks.com or scan this QR code. These links are routinely monitored and updated to provide the most current information available.

INDEX